PET OWNER'S GUIDE TO THE
DOBERMANN

Nancy & Clive Evans

RINGPRESS

ABOUT THE AUTHORS

Nancy Evans is a trained nurse and midwife who was born in Irvine, Ayrshire, where she grew up with dogs. Nancy's first experience with the Dobermann was through a family friend's two Dobermann bitches, Zeboo and Rhonda, who left a lasting impression that developed into the hobby which both Clive and Nancy enjoy today.

Clive has also had dogs all his life, including German Shepherds and Border Collies. Clive has daily contact with the general public and their animals through his job as a dog warden.

Nancy and Clive own the 'Amazon' affix, and are both Kennel Club approved

Clive Evans with Ch. Amazon Sound Machine.

Championship Show Judges. They have bred and owned 13 Dobermann UK and Irish Champions to date, and were top Dobermann breeders in 1990, 1997, 1998, 1999 and again in 2000.

Nancy and Clive owned the Crufts Best of Breed winner in 1997 and again in 1998 – Champion Amazon Sound Machine J.W. Ross, as he was known, was the Top Dobermann in 1997, Top Sire 1997 and Top Stud Dog 1998. At the present time, Ross has produced two UK Champions, and many more are well on their way to their UK title.

Cover: Shelley (Soduksky Simply The Best) owned by Cheryl Sproul, bred by Mr & Mrs Krafft.

Published by Ringpress Books Limited, PO Box 8, Lydney, Gloucestershire, GL15 4YN, United Kingdom.

Designed by Sarah Williams

First published 2001
©2001 Ringpress Books Limited. All rights reserved

ISBN 1 86054 114 3

Printed and bound in Hong Kong through Printworks International Ltd.

CONTENTS

SHOWING YOUR DOBERMANN 52

Ring training; The stand; Movement;
Type of show; Breed Standard (General
appearance; Size; Characteristics;
Temperament; Head and skull; Eyes;
Mouth; Neck; Body; Feet; Tail; Gait;
Colour).

BREEDING 58

Sire; Season/Heat; The mating; Post-
mating care; Checklist; Whelping box;
Bitch's temperature; Whelping; Post
whelping; Weaning; Potential owners;
Tails; Dewclaws; Nails.

HEALTH CARE 68

Parasites (Roundworms; Tapeworms; Heartworms; Fleas;
Mange Ticks); Accidents
(Burns; Cuts; Heat stroke;
Poisoning); Common
ailments (Bloat;
Cardiomyopathy; Eye
problems; Hip dysplasia;
Kennel cough; Parvovirus;
Pyometra; Von
Willebrand's Disease).

1 Introducing The Dobermann

The Dobermann is a relatively new breed, approximately 150 years old. There are no accurate records concerning the Dobermann, and there is a great deal of mystery surrounding the evolution of the breed as it is today. However, it is generally understood that a man called Herr Louis Dobermann from Apolda, in the state of Thuringia, Germany, is responsible for the breed, back in the mid-1880s.

Louis Dobermann was a tax collector, and therefore would have been very unpopular with local people. Considering the large amounts of cash he would be carrying while he was collecting taxes, he would have required a dog to be his companion and guard.

BREEDING PROGRAMME

The Dobermann is believed to be a combination of several dogs, which may include the Rottweiler, Beauceron, Manchester Terrier, Greyhound, and German Pinscher. Louis Dobermann was also reputed to have been a dog catcher, responsible for rounding up the local stray dogs.

Perhaps some of these strays were used to help develop his breeding programme. You can only imagine the many crossbreeds, mongrels and pure-bred dogs that found their way into Herr Dobermann's pound and how they provoked thoughts on how best these animals could be used to produce the ultimate guard and companion dog.

Herr Dobermann was a real dog fancier and his keen eye and dedication to improving and developing this beautiful breed allows us all to enjoy the Dobermann as it is today. He initially concentrated on a dog with strong guarding abilities, intelligence, a strong mouth (for

The Dobermann was bred to be intelligent and courageous, with plenty of stamina.

holding and restraining assailants until help became available), a good sense of smell (for tracking criminals and lost people or possessions), lots of courage and strength to ward off potentially difficult customers, and, above all else, loyalty. A short coat was needed as it would need little maintenance, and the dog also required a great deal of stamina, as Herr Dobermann travelled many miles with his various jobs.

Cropping the Dobermann's ears, a practice which takes place in some European countries and in the US (but not in the UK), was done to give the dog a more fierce and alert expression to ward off potential thieves. A more practical reason to crop or cut the ear was because the ears of these early Dobermanns were rather pendulous. When they were fighting or defending their owner, they were easily torn or ripped, so cropping became very popular.

FIRST BREED CLUB
In 1899, Otto Goeller, having

taken up the reins from Louis Dobermann, established the National Dobermann Pinscher Club. Together with some other club members, he set about producing the Dobermann Breed Standard (which is a written blueprint of the ideal Dobe). It was then that official acceptance was obtained by the club to the German Kennel Club.

TO THE UK

Dobermanns were first introduced to the UK in the early 1900s. The well-known judge, dog breeder, pony breeder and artist Lionel Hamilton-Renwick, along with Fred and Julia Curnow (Tavey kennels), were some of the first enthusiasts to import Dobermanns to the UK.

Lionel Hamilton-Renwick, of the Birling affix, imported a black and tan male, Birling Bruno v Ehrgarten from Switzerland. This male was bred by W. Lenz. Lionel Hamilton-Renwick was the breeder of the first male Dobermann Champion in the UK.

Fred Curnow was the chairperson of the Dobermann

Club, which was founded in 1948. The Dobermann Club was formerly called the Dobermann Pinscher Club. Another early member of the Dobermann Club was Sir Noel Curtis-Bennet, who was the first president.

TO THE US

The first Dobermann was imported from Germany into America by someone called E.R. Salmann in 1898. The first registered Dobe was Dobermann Intelectus in 1908.

In the USA and in some European countries, the ears are cropped.

WAR EFFORT

During the First World War, Dobermanns were used in the French Army as hospital dogs. They would search for wounded and dead soldiers that lay on the battlefield, and alert help.

Dobermanns were also used in the Second World War and proved a very successful all-round dog, attacking, guarding, and carrying and delivering items such as maps, medical supplies, telephone wires and explosives. These Dobes were trained to the highest of standards and shared the soldiers' lives in the muddy trenches. Also like the soldiers, they had to perform their tasks under dangerous conditions.

POLICE DOGS

Dobermanns have been used in the police force since the mid-1900s. A dog and a bitch were imported into the UK where the dog was taken over by Harry Darbyshire who was an officer in the dog section at the police headquarters in Guildford, Surrey. Prior to Mr. Darbyshire having the dog, his previous owner found him unmanageable and therefore gave him to Mr. Darbyshire to train as a police dog.

PINSCHER MOVEMENT

Up until 1957, the breed in the United Kingdom was more commonly known as the Dobermann Pinscher. From that date, the Kennel Club gave permission for the word 'Pinscher' to be dropped, as the literal translation of the word means 'terrier' and the Dobermann does not resemble a terrier in any shape or form.

FAMILY DOG

Despite their tough looks, Dobermanns are actually a very sensitive breed, and being over harsh or shouting too loudly will never be forgiven by your dog.

You do need to let your Dobermann know his or her place in the household pack, and that is at the bottom of it! Most Dobermanns will try to take advantage given the slightest encouragement, opportunity or weakness in their owners. They are most happy when they know their place, and they must not be allowed to be higher up the dominance scale than any member of your family, or any other human being, in fact (see Chapter Three).

BREED CHARACTER

The Dobermann is too clever for his own good sometimes, but there is no other breed like him in the world for loyalty and his endless sense of humour.

Dobermanns are very tactile and love to be the centre of attention. They can be real snobs one minute and complete idiots the next. They are very clever at appearing to be stupid when, in fact, they know exactly what they are doing.

Stubbornness is ingrained in the Dobermann psyche and is an essential part of the breed's make-up. With an enormous amount of patience, firmness and lots and lots of love and praise, a Dobermann can be a dream come true to own and show.

A good Dobermann has a very healthy respect of everything and everyone around him and, if treated well and socialised extensively, will give you very little trouble. You will have many happy memories from your Dobermann, and, with the right amount of love and discipline, he will be a treasure and a pleasure to own for many years to come.

Once he has learnt his place in the family pack, the Dobermann makes an ideal companion.

2 *The Dobermann Puppy*

There are a number of considerations before you decide to buy a Dobermann pup. Do you have enough time to dedicate to a new puppy? New puppies take up an enormous amount of time and patience.

With the extra work involved in caring for this newcomer, it can be likened to having a new baby in the house.

The amount of money that you will have to outlay on this new pup can be considerable. Pet insurance is a must for all new puppy owners, and you would be well advised to carry on the insurance cover given to you by the breeder of the puppy.

Feeding your new charge can cost a fair amount too, and all these considerations must be well looked into before you purchase your new friend.

FINDING A BREEDER

There are various ways of finding a new puppy. One way is to visit a Championship show near to where you live and enquire from the various exhibitors as to the availability of puppies. Advertisements in your local paper or the dedicated dog press are also worth investigating. Your national kennel club or breed club should have a puppy register with registered breeders listed. Word of mouth and recommendations from other breeders or by a vet is another way of finding a reputable breeder of good healthy stock.

PICKING A PUP

When you speak to a breeder do not be afraid to ask questions about the puppies, as I am sure he or she will have plenty to ask you! The questions you are likely to be asked are:

- Do you have someone at home all day to see to the puppy?
- Have you ever had a Dobermann before?
- Do you know how naughty and destructive they can be if left to their own devices?
- Is your garden totally secure and free from potential hazards?

A QUESTION OF SEX

Once you have satisfied each other's questions, the next step is to decide whether you would like to have a dog or a bitch puppy. Please take advice from the breeder on this as it may save you from making a mistake at this crucial time.

FEMALE

Female puppies may not always be better for the first-time pet owner due to the inconvenience of their seasons. Dobermann bitches usually come into season every six months for the whole of their lives.

During this time, extra vigilance

A bitch will need to be kept under strict supervision when she is in season.

The male has a strong physique and may present more of a training challenge

must be observed to ensure no misalliances take place while your bitch is vulnerable to local lotharios. You should not take her out until she has well and truly finished her season – about 21 to 25 days later.

If you already have a bitch, it is advisable that you stick to the same sex as Dobermann females generally get on well together.

However, extra care should be exercised around the time of their seasons as bitches can become temperamental as they may try to dominate each other due to the peaks and falls of hormones at this time.

MALE

Male animals can be a lot stronger both physically and mentally than females. This can be an advantage or a disadvantage depending on the type of person you are.

If you already have a male dog, no responsible breeder will sell you another. This is because male

Dobermanns generally will not tolerate one another – at some point there is likely to be a confrontation over who is dominant, and the inevitable fight will ensue.

A single male can be just as loving and faithful as a female. If you have trouble with the male cocking his leg and marking his territory (indoors as well as outdoors), ask your vet about castration.

VISITING THE LITTER

Now comes the time when you can go and see the new puppies. Look around to see how the

It is important to see the bitch with her puppies.

The breeder will help you to assess show potential.

puppies are housed and if they are clean and well fed. Make sure you see the mother and, if possible, any other members of the canine family that may be living there. They should have a friendly, outgoing disposition and come forward to see you with no sign of fear or fierceness. A Dobermann mother can be protective of her charges but if her owner has done his job, she will accept strangers viewing her babies reluctantly if not enthusiastically.

Look at the puppies for as long as you need, and do not be hurried into making a rushed choice – remember, this new puppy is going to be your companion for a very long time. The inquisitive puppy that is permanently trying to undo your shoelaces is normally a good bet in the confidence race.

PHYSICAL TRAITS

Make sure that the males look masculine, and the females feminine! The legs must be well boned and straight, ending in tight cat-like feet. The rear legs of the puppy, when viewed from behind, must be straight and firm, with a nice clean tail-set which should be a continuation of the spine.

Look at the pup's head and observe if he has an alert expression with dark eyes that are full of mischief and ready for anything. His coat should be shiny and sleek, with rich rust-coloured markings.

PUPPY-PROOFING

Your garden should be puppy-proofed to prevent your pup from escaping and from causing damage to himself. Ensure that garden gates are kept securely closed and locked at all times except when in use. A spring-loaded hinge on your garden gate will be of great use if you have young children around who may forget to shut the gate behind them. Ensure that your puppy is unable to squeeze underneath any gates or fencing.

If your garden is big enough, you may decide to puppy-proof one area, such as a patio. You may also decide to fence off a special area (dog run) that your puppy can be put into. The fence should be at least four feet (1.5 metres) high and sturdy enough to prevent your puppy from pushing it over in his efforts to escape confinement, or chase your neighbour's cat.

Take stock of what plants you have in your garden, as some of them could be poisonous to your new puppy, or, at the very least, give him a tummy upset.

Make sure you spend some time puppy-proofing your house, too. All electrical cables and equipment must be made inaccessible. Hanging table cloths or long curtains are a great temptation to your new puppy and should be lifted or removed from his reach.

Common sense must be used at all time; anything valuable or delicate must be removed or put out of your puppy's reach – if you do not, then you have no one to blame but yourself for any damage caused. A puppy playpen is a good investment (see page 20), and will safeguard both your puppy and your possessions.

JOURNEY HOME

Make sure you receive a diet sheet for the puppy, and the breeder should also supply you with enough food for a couple of days until you can buy some of your own.

Equip yourself for the journey home with newspapers, kitchen-roll, wet-wipes and a blanket and towel for the comfort of yourself and the new puppy. If he or she is to sit on your lap on the way home, these items will be useful if the new puppy is sick, or has a toileting accident. If you are collecting the pup on your own, you will have to put the pup in a pet carrier cage in the car. Make sure that it is not too big for the puppy, or he will be thrown about during the journey.

Your puppy will feel bewildered when he first arrives in his new home.

ARRIVING HOME

Once you have safely reached home, do not let the puppy become overwhelmed with too many people wanting to see and stroke him. Let him adjust to his surroundings quietly and slowly. I am sure you will remember your first day at school or at a new job and how insecure you might have been, well it's the same for your puppy.

The first thing your puppy will need to do is to relieve himself, especially if the journey has been a long one! Next, show your puppy where his bed is. Make sure it is as comfortable for him as possible and away from any draughts. A warm, washable blanket with a few of his toys at hand will help him settle into his new surroundings. Encourage him to spend a few minutes in his bed by stroking him, and gently talking to him as he gradually relaxes and accepts his new bedroom.

FAMILY INTRODUCTIONS

Introduce your puppy gradually to other pets. Cats will tolerate him only at their own pace. Make sure that there is room for your pet cat or dog to get away from the newcomer. A small barrier or puppy playpen that keeps your puppy in and allows your other pet to get away may prove a good investment in the long run.

Do not allow children or pets to associate with the new puppy unless they are properly supervised

To begin with, your puppy will miss the companionship of his brothers and sisters.

and do not let small children crowd or maul young puppies at any time.

Puppies need mutual respect and consideration from their young playmates, and, if given the right training to both the puppy and the child, will grow up to be the best of friends and will probably become inseparable.

When your puppy is sleeping make sure he is never disturbed. Do not allow young children to wake him up just so they can play. Puppies need a great deal of sleep, so leave him alone – when he wakes up, there will be plenty of time for fun and games for everyone.

Encourage your children to get involved with the day-to-day care of the new puppy, as feeding, grooming and training will all help to create a bond with the whole family and is an excellent basis for the future of the whole household.

Teach your children how to hold the puppy, i.e. putting one arm under his bottom and one around his chest. If the puppy feels safe, he will not struggle.

However, do not allow very young children to lift the puppy up, as a dropped puppy can result in unnecessary injuries.

FIRST NIGHT

At bedtime, a radio left playing at low volume will stop him feeling quite so alone through the night, and a hot-water bottle wrapped up in a towel or blanket will give him something to cuddle up to in the night. Make sure you leave him dry newspapers to relieve himself on. Put them in the place where, until he is fully toilet-trained, you would like him to perform (e.g. by the back door).

It is not unusual to have a few sleepless nights when you first have your new puppy, so don't be too impatient and annoyed with him. Go down after about 10 to 15 minutes, reassure him, and leave him to settle quietly and eventually he will go off to sleep.

Do not make the mistake of allowing your cute little puppy to share your bed as this little puppy will soon turn into a 90-lb adult that will gradually start to take over more than his share of your bed.

Allow your puppy to sleep as much as he wants. It is a well-known adage that when your puppy is asleep he is doing most of his growing, and of course it leaves you free to get on with your housework or whatever else needs doing when you are not entertaining the little darling.

Do not let young children disturb the puppy when he is resting. There will be plenty of time to play once the puppy has awakened of his own accord, and he will be more than ready to oblige the children.

TOILET-TRAINING

When trying to house-train your puppy there are a few golden rules. First thing in the morning, take him outside and watch until he relieves himself. When he has performed, really praise him and make a big fuss of him. You can also give him a treat to reinforce his good behaviour.

Repeat this procedure at the following times:

- After he has awoken from sleep.
- After he has finished his meal.
- Approximately every two hours, gradually increasing the length of time until he may only need to go out every three hours or so.
- Before he is put to bed for the night.

If he does happen to have an accident, place him outside to finish his misdemeanour. He will eventually learn that the outdoors is the place for performing. Do not be tempted in the heat of the moment to smack or lash out in anger, otherwise you will have to go back to square one in the trust department. Hands should always be used to reinforce love, kindness, and reassurance for a puppy, never to punish.

PAPER-TRAINING

Confine your puppy to a small, 'puppy-proofed' room and paper the entire floor. Put his bed, toys and food/water bowls there. At first, he will probably play with the papers, chew on them, and drag them around his little den.

While your puppy is confined, he will develop a habit of eliminating on paper because, no matter where he goes, it will be on paper. As time goes on, he will start to show a preferred place to do his business.

When this place is established and the rest of the papers remain clean all day, then gradually reduce the area that is papered. Start removing the paper that is furthest away from his chosen location. Eventually, you will only need to leave a few sheets down in that area only. If he misses the

Allocate an area in the garden to use for toilet-training.

paper, it means you have reduced the area too soon. Go back to papering a larger area or even the entire room.

Once your pup is reliably going only on the papers you've left, then you can slowly and gradually move his papers to a location of your choice (such as closer to the back door, and then, eventually, out into the garden). Move the papers only a couple of inches a day. If he misses the paper again, then you're moving too fast. Go back a few steps and start over.

The most important thing you

can do to make house-training happen as quickly as possible is to reward and praise your puppy every time he goes in the right place. The more times he is rewarded, the quicker he will learn. Therefore, it's important that you spend as much time as possible with your pup and give him regular and frequent access to his toilet area.

There will always be minor setbacks, but if you stick with this procedure, your puppy will be paper-trained.

POOP-SCOOPS
It is unhygienic and unsociable not to clean up after your dog and in most places it is illegal not to do so. All dog owners have the same responsibilities, and this includes scooping the poop! If you don't like the mess, imagine how others feel when your dog fouls.

Here are four tips:
- If your dog fouls, always clean it up immediately.
- Encourage your dog to foul in your garden before he is taken out for exercise.
- Always carry something to clean up after your dog.
- Try to avoid letting your dog foul where children play, or where people play sports.

- Scooping up will help prevent infection to others.

FEEDING
You should keep the puppy on the same food that he was reared on to save any tummy upsets that a change could cause. If you want to change his food, talk to the breeder. A change of diet must only be done once the pup has settled into his new home, and it must be performed gradually, mixing the new food in with the food he has been used to, and reducing the amount of the former food until a complete change-over has been completed.

We always feed our pups the following menu.

SAMPLE MENU
Complete puppy food, soaked with warm water, with a small amount of cooked minced lamb, beef or chicken. Refer to the manufacturer's recommended food amounts. Always tailor the amount of food to your individual puppy – some may need more food than others of the same age and breed.

The same can be fed for lunch, dinner, and supper. Sometimes, I replace meat with scrambled eggs, tuna or live yoghurt for their

Feed the diet your puppy has been used to during his settling-in period.

dinner. Goat or diluted cow's milk can be given as a water replacement after your puppy has eaten his meal. Fresh, clean water should be available at all times.

Vary the amounts of food offered according to the appetite of your puppy.

- At two to three months, four meals to be offered daily.
- At four to five months, three meals to be offered daily.
- From six months onwards, two meals to be offered daily.

If your puppy is reluctant to eat for a few days after you bring him home, it will probably be due to the upset of leaving his littermates. Dogs and puppies will eat when they are hungry, and unless they look ill or depressed, leave them to their own devices until they are ready. If he continues to refuse food, or if you are at all concerned, consult a vet.

CRATE-TRAINING

Teach your puppy that his crate/cage is a safe and welcoming place. Make sure it is of adequate size for the fully-grown adult to be able to stand up and turn around comfortably. The ideal size is roughly 32 inches high by 27 inches wide by 40 inches long (80 x 67.5 x 100 cms).

A comfortable piece of washable bedding should be placed in the bottom of the crate for the puppy to sleep on. Make sure the crate/cage comes with a removable, washable tray on the bottom for ease of cleaning, as your puppy will inevitably have a few accidents when he starts being trained in his crate.

Allow the puppy free access to the crate. Put a few of his toys and chewies inside, and encourage him to sleep in it. Feeding your puppy in his cage will also help him associate the crate with a nice place.

At first, leave the door open. After a few days, close the door for 10 minutes, gradually building up to 1 hour. After a few weeks, your puppy will associate the crate with a safe place and will make it his home and look forward to spending his time in there.

Never shut your pup in the crate for long periods of time, or use it as a 'prison', confining him in it if he has been naughty.

CHEWING

All puppies chew, and nothing in your home will be sacred – carpets, wood, furniture, the list is endless and can be very expensive. Please remember that this destruction is not your puppy's fault. Make sure that you leave adequate toys and bones (not chicken, lamb or pork bones) or a nylon chew stick, for your puppy to play with and to occupy his time (and to save you a fortune in damaged possessions!).

There are various types of chews on the market, some are safe and some can be dangerous. The safest are the non-edible ones, the most dangerous are usually the prettiest. Read the instructions on the toy or chew before you buy it for your puppy.

Although puppies can chew them, they should never be able to bite them into small, digestible pieces or they could get trapped in the throat, stomach and intestines, which is very dangerous. With rawhides, the bigger they are, the better. You must always supervise your pup with his chews at all times.

EXERCISE

Before you take your puppy out into the big wide world, he must be fully covered by his inoculations. You must *never* allow your puppy out to mix with any other dogs until his inoculations are fully complete. It is never worth the heartache of possibly

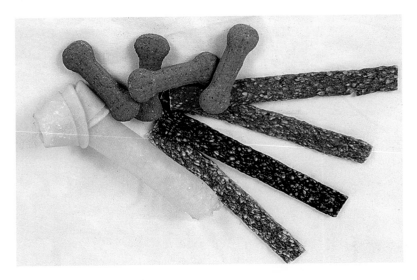

Provide suitable chews for your puppy, especially when he is teething.

losing your dog just because you couldn't patiently wait a few weeks. Until he is inoculated, restrict exercise to your garden.

Initially, your young puppy will only need about 10 to 15 minutes, lead-exercise twice a day for the first four months of his life (see Lead-training, Chapter Five). The rest of the time he will get enough exercise by running around and playing in your garden.

As your puppy gets older allow him 10 to 15 minutes' free running in a secure fenced area, to help him get rid of some energy before you embark on a slow road-walk for around 20 to 40 minutes. Slow road-walking encourages your dog to use all his muscles in the desired manner, allowing the muscles in his forequarters and hindquarters to develop in the correct way. This is of great advantage to both the family pet and the ultimate Champion show dog.

Once he has reached about six months of age, you can gradually increase the amount of exercise given to suit both his and your needs.

GENTLY DOES IT
Remember that your puppy is a rapidly developing youngster and

Lead-walking should be kept to short sessions.

you should not exceed exercise in any shape or form, however tempting, as you will ultimately succeed in doing more harm than good.

- Do not let your puppy run up and down the stairs. This can cause damage to their developing bones.

- Steep banks and numerous steps have also to be avoided for the same reason.
- Lift your puppy into and out of the tailgate of your car, again to avoid unnecessary stress on his developing joints and bones.
- Never lift your puppy by the front legs; always place your

hand under his rear and around his chest when you have to lift him for any reason.

IDENTIFICATION

Permanent identification may already have been given to a young puppy before it leaves the breeder and may be in the form of a tattoo in the inside of the pup's ear. This tattoo will be a unique combination of a few numbers and letters. The owner's details will be held on a database that is run by a registration company for the purpose of tattoo identification.

Permanent identification may also be in the form of a microchip that is implanted under the skin on the neck. The microchip itself is approximately the size of a grain of rice and will be unable to be detected without the use of a scanner. When a microchipped

Do not over-exercise a young puppy as his bones and joints are very vulnerable while he is growing.

Microchipping is an invisible way to safeguard against losing your puppy.

dog is scanned, a microchip with a series of numbers and letters can be detected. Again, the owner's details will be held on a database run by a registration company.

A microchip has the advantage that it cannot be tampered with, unlike a tattoo. Tattoos can also become illegible after a few years. Some people are concerned that a microchip may migrate to other parts of the body, but, if implanted correctly, it should not.

SOCIALISATION

As with any breed, socialisation is a vitally important part of training your puppy. Many clubs and vets now hold puppy parties, to enable young dogs to meet other breeds and learn to develop their social skills.

Take your puppy everywhere you can, including a town centre, local pub, and other places where your puppy will be in contact with lots of people. This will allow him access to all manner of everyday stimuli and experiences.

Owning a fully-grown Dobermann who is anti-social or

uncontrollable, is not only embarrassing, but dangerous. Therefore, it is important to introduce your young puppy to other dogs and people to enable him to be confident with as many situations as possible.

For information on training your Dobe pup and adult, see Chapter Four.

When your puppy is fully inoculated, take him out and about as much as possible.

3

The Adult Dobermann

An adult Dobermann is quite an easy breed to care for. However, although he needs little grooming etc., he will still need considerable exercise and lots of training to keep his mind occupied and to increase his bond with his owners (see Chapter Four).

FAMILY RULES

The Dobermann will play by the rules, as long as he knows them. The main rule is that he is bottom of the family pack. He must understand that you and your family are the pack leaders and that he must respect you at all times.

He may try to assert his dominance by barking, growling, or attempting to bite. It is obviously easier to rectify dominance while a dog is young, as you can discipline him when he does something wrong, and praise him when he does well.

I can recall the first time that one of my dogs tried to be dominant. I went to take marrowbone off a 14-week-old pup, and he attempted to bite me. I had to reprimand him, and teach him that if someone wants to take something from him, they are absolutely allowed to, and should be shown no aggression at all. I regularly gave the pup a bone, and took it away again to reinforce this idea.

EXERCISE

When they reach maturity, fully-grown Dobermanns require a minimum of one hour's hard walking/free-running each day, every day. If you don't think you could manage to exercise your dog this much, the Dobermann is not the dog for you.

In winter, take care to ensure your dog is dried off properly when he returns from his daily walks. A little coconut oil or baby oil applied to any dry areas will help to relieve any soreness.

An adult Dobermann needs a varied programme of exercise.

RESCUE DOGS

There are many Dobermanns in rescue societies throughout the world, and you may like to consider rehoming one.

Before taking one on, enquire why the dog is in rescue, and ascertain as much information about the dog's background as possible. Some rescue Dobes come with their own set of problems – usually as a result of unsuitable owners. Before taking on such a dog, be prepared to give a lot of time, effort and love.

Most rescue societies will allow you to spend time with a dog, so you can be certain of your compatibility before taking him home. There is usually a trial period, too, and most rescues insist that if it does not work out, for whatever reason, that the dog is returned to them for rehoming.

COAT CARE

A Dobermann's coat should be smooth-haired, short (about 2cm), hard, thick and close-lying. Invisible grey undercoat on the neck is permissible in the show ring, but hair forming a ridge on the back of the neck/spine should be classed as a serious fault.

As with most other breeds, Dobermanns shed their hair, so will require regular grooming. Using a stippled rubber glove you will be able to remove dead hair, stimulate blood supply to the skin, and so keep the skin healthy.

Baby wipes are a godsend to Dobermann owners. These soft, moist, very mild tissues are very good for giving your Dobermann a daily wipe over and they make him smell sweeter too.

Grooming gives you the opportunity to examine your Dobermann all over, enabling you to find any lumps or scratches that may have gone unnoticed. Grooming also helps to increase the closeness with your dog.

As with all dogs, a Dobermann will produce natural oils, which protect the coat and will make it shine. A correctly balanced diet will also contribute to your dog's condition.

BITCH'S COAT

Many Dobermann bitches tend to lose their hair on the loin area. This is mainly due to a hormonal imbalance, and therefore it is best to consult a veterinary surgeon. He or she may administer hormone replacement tablets in the form of thyroxin that will need to be administered for the rest of the dog's life.

Grooming provides a good opportunity to examine your Dobermann.

BATHING

Your Dobermann should not need very much bathing. If your dog smells unpleasant or has rolled in mud (or worse), put him in the bath and shower him, wetting the coat thoroughly. Use a very mild shampoo or one recommended by your vet or local grooming parlour. Massage it into the coat, lathering it up nicely, and being sure to avoid the eyes. Rinse thoroughly.

Make sure your Dobermann is dried properly, especially under the armpits and on the under side of the abdomen as these areas can become red, sore and irritated if left damp.

EARS

It is important to check your dog for any signs of ear disorders, as early detection can prevent the spread of infection to the middle and inner ear.

Ears should be cleaned at least once a week. Using moist cotton wool (cotton), clean away any visible amounts of ear wax, being careful not to go too deep into the ear canal. Never use anything hard to clean the ear, such as cotton buds.

If you notice that the ears are red and inflamed, you should consult a vet for treatment. Any smelly, dark secretions (commonly called canker) in the ears should be wiped away carefully and a special ear-cleaning fluid applied as directed by the manufacturer. These ear drops and cleaners are specially formulated to clear canker and to kill any ear mites. Used regularly, they will prevent re-infestation or infection.

NAILS

Nails need to be kept trimmed, as long nails can make the dog's feet go flat and unsightly. If the nails are left to grow, they can cause injury, such as being broken off or torn out at the root if they get caught in something. Your vet will

Filing nails is often more acceptable than clipping.

clip and trim the nails for you, but if you feel competent, you may wish to clip/trim the nails yourself.

Be warned that most Dobermanns' nails are black or dark brown in colour and you will be unable to see the quick (the blood supply that grows within the nail). Be careful not to cut the quick, as this will cause the dog's nail to bleed and cause the dog some pain.

An alternative to clipping the nails is to file them, something which Dobermanns seem to tolerate more readily, often falling asleep while having their feet manicured.

FEET

Check your dog's feet regularly for any cracks, cuts or sores on the pad, or between the toes. Minor cuts or sores should be treated with a small amount of barrier cream. Anything more serious should be seen by a vet.

CARING FOR THE VETERAN

Dobermanns live to approximately 10 to 12 years of age. They grow old gracefully, and some of the first signs are usually a few grey hairs around the muzzle. You may notice a general slowing up of your pet, especially when he is out on walks.

Veterans are wonderful. They know your every move, and you know them well enough to trust them completely. They still like to feel involved in family activities.

Never forget that your veteran is still a valuable member of your household. My oldies have taught my youngsters many manners and important lessons. They are invaluable members of our household and are treasured.

When it comes to feeding, don't be tempted to overfeed your veteran – they like to act as if they have never been fed in their lives before and love to prick your conscience in the food stakes. Our oldies will almost perform somersaults in an attempt to bribe you into giving them that extra little treat, but it is important to keep an eye on your dog's weight, as obesity can be seriously detrimental to health.

Allow your veteran all the peace and quiet that he wants and don't allow him to be plagued by any overenthusiastic youngsters (canine and human) that may try to bother them. Give him a quiet place of his own that he can retreat to if he so wishes.

Make sure your Dobermann receives regular check-ups with your vet. This will ensure that minor ailments will be spotted and treated before they become too big a problem.

SAYING GOODBYE

Euthanasia (putting your companion to sleep) is something that most dog owners will have to experience at some time in their lives. It is something that you will have to think about before you have your new puppy, as sadly not all dogs die of old age in their sleep. Euthanasia is the last great act of love that we can give our sick and suffering pet, if his suffering far outweighs the pain of being parted from us, no matter how much it hurts us.

You can ask your veterinary surgeon to carry out this service for you and your companion in your own home, if he is agreeable. This may be more acceptable than taking your friend to unfamiliar surroundings to say your last goodbyes.

The procedure consists of an overdose injection of anaesthesia or barbiturate that is usually injected into the main bloodstream via a vein in a foreleg. Your dog will feel no

The veteran still enjoys being part of family activities.

Be prepared to let go when the time comes, and look back on all the happy times you and your Dobermann spent together.

more than a slight prick when the injection is being administered and will be asleep before it is completed.

Your vet will need to know if you want your companion's body returned to you for burial in your own garden or if you would like the body to be disposed of by them. You may also decide to have your companion cremated and the ashes returned to you in an urn or casket; this can be arranged by your vet.

Training Your Dobermann

Dobermanns love to work. They need mental as well as physical exercise, so if you do not have the time or energy to give to training your Dobermann, you should consider getting another breed!

Due to some bad press and poor public opinion which this breed has had, it is now more than ever vital that you train your Dobermann. The breed is headstrong and needs firm (not hard) control.

It is vital to be consistent with the training of your young and adult Dobermann and you must ensure that all your family are involved in the dog's training so he learns to respect you all.

THE RIGHT ATTITUDE

Because Dobermanns are such an intelligent breed and very much have a mind of their own, they are not a breed for the weak-willed or impatient. You need to be consistent in your training and discipline in order to gain respect from your Dobermann. You must be of a secure, confident personality; if you are in any way unsure of how to control or train your dog, he will sense it and will start to treat you with contempt.

However, hard handling can make for a shy, cautious animal which is as much of a danger as an over-confident dog. As with all dogs, a combination of love and discipline is important, and there is a very fine line between being too hard and too soft. It is finding the right balance that determines how successful you are in training and owning this beautiful breed.

TRAINING METHODS

Dobermanns are very easy to train, are incredibly quick learners, and because they are usually very focused on their owners, they want to please. This makes them a joy to train.

There are two types of training: positive (reward-based) and

Dobermanns are quick learners and are generally eager to please.

negative (punitive). Reward-based training is the most effective, and is based on rewarding your Dobe every time he does something that you want. For example, if your dog barks, and you tell him "Quiet!", and he falls silent, you should immediately reward him. Rewards include treats, petting, verbal praise, and play.

Correct or prevent the bad behaviour – don't punish the puppy. Teaching and communication is what it's all about, not getting even with your dog. If you're taking an "it's-you-against-him, knock him into

shape" approach, you'll undermine your relationship, while missing out on all the fun that a motivational training approach can offer.

GOOD TIMING

When training your puppy, whether praising or correcting, good timing is essential. Take the following example: you've prepared a platter of sandwiches for lunch, which you've left on your kitchen counter. Your dog walks into the room and smells the sandwiches. He air-sniffs, then eyes the food, and is poised to jump up. This is the best, easiest and most effective time to correct your dog: before he's misbehaved, while he's thinking about jumping up to get the food. Stay one step ahead, and try to think of what your puppy is going to do before he does, and correct him before he does it. Often, dog owners inadvertently reinforce their puppy's misbehaviour by giving their pup lots of attention when they are naughty. If your puppy receives lots of attention and handling when he jumps up on you, that behaviour is being reinforced, and is therefore likely to be repeated. The simple rule is: ignore inappropriate behaviour and reward the good.

Keep your commands simple so that your puppy understands what is required.

TRAINING CLASSES

As soon as your pup has had his vaccinations, you should enrol at a training class. Dobermanns thrive on being kept mentally alert, so a good training club (not just one that teaches your dog to heel and sit at the roadside) should be able to help with exercises to keep your dog alert and focused on you.

GIVING COMMANDS

Avoid giving your dog commands that you cannot enforce. Every time you give a command that is neither complied with nor enforced, he will soon learn that commands are optional.

One command should equal one response, so only give your dog one command (twice

Keep training sessions short, and make sure your puppy enjoys them.

maximum!). Then, gently enforce it. Repeating commands will teach your dog that the first command is a 'bluff' and not really meant. For instance, telling your dog to "Sit, sit, sit, sit!" is neither an efficient nor effective way to issue commands. Simply give your dog a command, "Sit", and gently place or lure your dog into the required position, then quietly praise/reward him.

Avoid giving combined commands, which are confusing to your puppy. Combined commands such as "Sit-down" can confuse your puppy. Using this example, say either "Sit" or "Down".

TONE OF VOICE

When giving your puppy a command, avoid using a loud voice. Even if your puppy is especially independent or unresponsive, your tone of voice when issuing an obedience command should be calm and assertive, rather than harsh or loud. Many owners complain that their dogs are stubborn and that they refuse to listen when given a command. Before blaming the puppy when he doesn't respond to a command, one must determine whether or not:

a) the pup knows what the owner wants.
b) he knows how to comply.
c) he is not simply being unresponsive due to fear, stress or confusion.

PUPPY TRAINING

Training essentially begins the minute that you arrive home with your new puppy. During the first six months of a dog's life behavioural problems can develop that, if left uncorrected, can last a lifetime. By using gentle training methods you can guide your puppy in the right direction, avoiding many of the problems that he would otherwise develop.

While older dogs can be taught new tricks, what they learn early, is often learned quickest and easiest. Moreover, the older the dog, the more bad habits there are that need to be 'un-learned'. When it comes to raising and training a dog, an ounce of problem prevention is certainly worth a pound of cure!

EARLY LESSONS

Firstly, you will need to teach your new puppy his name (tip: keep it short and sweet). Through repetition, your pup will recognise his name and answer to it.

Whenever possible, use your puppy's name positively, rather than using it in conjunction with reprimands, warnings or punishment. Your puppy should trust that, when he hears his name or is called to you, good things happen. His name should always be a word he responds to with enthusiasm, never hesitancy or fear. This is the first stage of training.

The next stage in training is to command your puppy whenever he does something naturally, such as sits, lies down, comes to you, etc. A young puppy will soon learn commands you give, as long as the commands are always the same, i.e. Sit, Lie, and Come.

During training, you should attract your puppy's attention by saying his name and then giving a command. People have been heard giving their dog a command and then saying his name. This will confuse the dog.

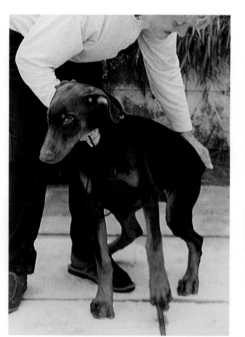
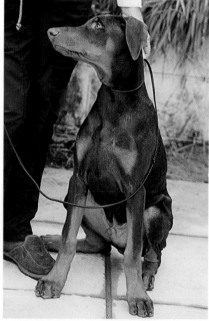

If necessary, apply gentle pressure to the hindquarters to encourage your puppy into the Sit.

Give the command "Down" as your puppy goes into the correct position.

There are five basic commands: Sit, Down/Lie, Stay, Wait, and Come.

SIT

To teach your dog to sit on command, hold a tidbit in one hand, positioned in front of your dog's nose. With your other hand, gently push down on the rear end of your dog. While pressing down on your dog's rear, slowly move the tidbit up and towards your dog. While doing all that, give an assertive verbal command such as "Sit". When he sits, give him the tidbit, and make a big fuss of him, so he feels as if he is very clever indeed.

DOWN/LIE

Start with your puppy in the Sit position (above). Now place your left hand on your puppy's shoulders and gently push down. Holding a tidbit in your right hand, ark it downwards, allowing your puppy to keep his nose close to it, until your hand is on the floor and a short distance in front of the puppy. While carrying out these procedures, again give your puppy an assertive verbal command such as "Down" or "Lie". Your puppy should now have his belly on the floor. As soon as he achieves this Down position, give him the treat and lots of praise.

Build up the Stay exercise in simple stages.

STAY

Teach your puppy that when you say "Stay!" he is required to stay where he is told until another command is given. Again, start in the Sit position with a lead attached to your puppy. While holding the lead vertically above your puppy's head, command him to Stay and then step away one pace, keeping the lead above his head. If your puppy tries to break the command, you should be able to control him with the use of the lead. At first, only allow your puppy to stay in one position for a moment or two until he becomes accustomed to the exercise. When your puppy successfully stays while you are close by, then you can start to extend your distance from him. We recommend that your puppy is always trained in a confined area such as your garden and that he is kept held on a lead.

WAIT
This command is similar to Stay except you will give your dog a second command. For example, if you are waiting to cross a road, most people will command their dog to "Sit" and then command it to "Stay". The correct command should be "Sit" and "Wait", you will then break the Wait command when you command your dog to "Walk on".

COME
This command needs no interpretation except to say that when you command your dog to Come, he will come to you, wherever you are – indoors or out.

To teach this exercise, call your dog's name and then give the comand "Come!". Once the dog

has returned to you, give him a tidbit. With practice, your dog will soon realise that when he comes when called, he is rewarded with treats and praise.

Remember not to let your dog off the leash in a public place until his recall is perfect – if your dog doesn't respond reliably to commands at home (where distractions are relatively minimal), he certainly won't respond to you outdoors where other dogs, cats, birds, farm animals or even other people can tempt him.

LEAD-TRAINING
Lead training should not be too difficult if you start when your Dobermann is still a young pup. Introduce your Dobe to wearing his collar as soon as he has settled into his new home. Some breeders may have introduced the puppy to wearing a light collar or even a coloured shoestring for identification purposes. A soft, adjustable nylon collar is the best collar to start with; leave it on him for a short period initially, gradually increasing the time until he is comfortable with the idea of wearing it.

Put his lead on the collar and allow him to walk around with

The aim is to have your Dobermann walking calmly to heel on a loose lead.

the lead attached but without you holding the end of it. Gradually start to pick up the lead and, with the help of a friend and an occasional tidbit, encourage the pup to walk forward with a slight amount of pressure from you on the end of the lead. Try this a few times until the puppy feels no threat from the lead and will walk comfortably with you.

Patience and calmness at all times are needed as your puppy may not like this kind of restraint. With plenty of praise and encouragement, he will eventually come round to your way of thinking,

associating his lead with enjoyable walks and family outings.

When your pup is walking nicely beside you, say "Heel" and he will learn to associate the word with the action. Praise your puppy in abundance when he has performed well, and ignore him when he misbehaves.

There is nothing worse than seeing an adult Dobermann taking his owner for a walk, so be patient and consistent in your training, and, if you feel you need help, do not be afraid to ask for it – there are numerous puppy classes you can attend.

OBEDIENCE

The intelligent Dobermann is extremely good at Obedience and has a natural ability to undertake Obedience competition work.

If you decide to take up competitive Obedience work, you will need to be dedicated and willing to spend a lot of time on regular training. Many people think that all they need to do is attend a class, once a week, but training should be done every day, incorporated into your daily routines.

Obedience work can be very beneficial to you and your dog, as it will bond you and your dog closer together. Remember that a well-trained dog is a happy dog.

AGILITY

Dobes also enjoy competing in Agility. This is where dogs are sent over jumps, under obstacles, through tunnels and tyres, over seesaws and through weaving stakes. Some dogs get bored very quickly, especially with repetitive tasks, so their training work should be varied and challenging – make sure there is plenty of play, and lots of time out!

If you wish to join an Obedience or Agility training club, contact your local dog warden, veterinary practice, and your national kennel club, who should be able to provide you with details of accredited trainers in your area.

Ch. Amazon Brahm's N Lizt JW: Winner of 24 Challenge Certificates, and Top Dobermann for three years.

5 *Showing Your Dobermann*

If you decide to show your Dobermann, you firstly need to establish whether your dog is of show quality. Tell the breeder, when you first enquire about a puppy, exactly what you want. Most breeders will be more than happy to help you to select a promising pup.

Do not be over-confident of your pup developing into a future Champion, however. Breeding is not an exact science, and no matter how promising a puppy is, things can go wrong before he is six months – he may grow too big, or lack an essential quality necessary in the show ring.

RING TRAINING
Ring training prepares your dog for the show ring. It teaches your Dobe to stand in a show pose and to allow any person (i.e. the judge) to examine him all over. During ring training, you will be taught how to move/gait your dog at the correct speed (trot), and the correct ring procedures.

THE STAND
It is advisable to train your dog for the show ring as early as possible by standing your young pup on a low table. In the UK, owners often encourage pups to

stand by keeping their attention on a treat. In some other countries, however, a fine cord collar is used around the neck to hold the pup in place while placing the legs into the correct position.

The front legs should be vertical and the rear hocks vertical when viewed from behind. Both the front and rear legs should be parallel when viewed from the front or rear.

When in the show ring, the judge will be looking at your dog from different angles to observe the dog's overall construction in accordance with the Breed Standard.

MOVEMENT

After the judge has examined your Dobermann to check his conformation, he will then ask you to move/gait (trot) your dog around the ring. The judge will ask you to move your dog in a particular pattern (e.g. up and down, or in a triangle). The judge will be looking for good extension of the front legs, with no noticeable toeing in or out of the front feet. The hind legs should have a powerful drive with rotary action when the dog is viewed in profile. The dog's back must remain strong and firm when moving at all times.

TYPE OF SHOW

There are many different types of show; from fun shows held at your local fête, through to the top Championship shows, such as Crufts in the UK and Westminster in the US. Ask the advice of your dog's breeder as to where you should start out. It is useful to have someone who knows the show world who can talk you through all the different classes and rules and regulations. However, the more you get

Competition is intense at Championship level.

The Dobermann combines strength with elegance.

involved, the more it will all seem much simpler.

Details of forthcoming shows are advertised in the dog press.

BREED STANDARD

Before you even consider showing your Dobermann, of course, you must make sure he is a good example of the breed, and that he closely resembles the ideal Dobe described in the Breed Standard.

GENERAL APPEARANCE

The Dobermann is a medium-sized dog, muscular and elegant with a strong body, and capable of a swift turn of foot.

SIZE

The ideal height of a Dobermann at the shoulders should be as follows:
- Males 69 cm (27 in)
- Females 65 cm (25½ in)

In reality there is a variation of up to approximately 5 cm (2 in).

CHARACTERISTICS

The Dobermann should be intelligent and firm of character, loyal and obedient.

TEMPERAMENT

He should be bold and alert. There should be no signs of shyness or viciousness.

The head should be clean-cut and balanced.

HEAD AND SKULL

The head and skull should be balanced and in proportion to the size of the body. The head should be long, well filled out under the eyes, and clean cut, with a good depth of muzzle. Seen from above and from the side, the head resembles an elongated blunt wedge. The upper part of the head should be flat and free from wrinkle. The cheeks should be flat, and the lips tight. The nose should be solid black in black dogs, solid dark brown in brown dogs, solid dark-grey in blue dogs, and light brown in fawn dogs.

EYES

The eyes should be almond-shaped, with a lively, alert expression. The colour of the eyes should be uniform, ranging from medium to darkest brown in black dogs, the darker shade being more desirable. In browns, blues, or fawns, the colour of the iris blends with that of the markings, but should not be of a lighter hue than the markings; light eyes in black dogs are highly undesirable.

MOUTH

The mouth should be well developed, solid and strong, with complete dentition and a perfect, regular and complete scissor-bite (i.e. the upper teeth closely overlapping the lower teeth and set square to the jaws). The teeth should be evenly placed.

NECK

The neck should be fairly long and lean, carried with considerable nobility. The shape should be lightly convex and in proportion to the shape of dog. The nape region should be very muscular.

BODY

The body should be square in profile. The chest should be well developed and full. The back should be short and firm, with strong, straight topline sloping slightly.

FEET

They should be tight and well bunched like a cat's foot.

TAIL

Customarily docked at first or second joint. The tail appears to be a continuation of spine without any noticeable drop.

GAIT

Elastic, free, balanced and vigorous, with good reach in the forequarters and driving power in the hindquarters. Rear and front legs thrown neither in nor out. The back remains strong and firm.

COLOUR

Definite black, brown, blue or fawn (Isabella) only, with rust-red markings. Markings to be sharply defined, appearing above each eye, on the muzzle, the throat and the fore chest, on all legs and feet, and below tail. White markings of any kind are highly undesirable.

The Dobermann colours (left to right): Brown, black, fawn, Isabella, and blue, all with rust-red markings.

6 *Breeding*

Before you even consider breeding, ask yourself the following questions:
- Can I afford it?
- Do I have adequate room?
- Do I have the time?
- Who will I mate my dog/bitch to?
- Will I be able to find homes for the puppies?
- Will I need a licence to breed?

Health must be one of the most important factors when mating a bitch.
- She should be free of parasites (e.g. worm-free).
- Her inoculations should be up to date and she should be infection-free.
- She should have been tested for all breed-specific conditions (ask your vet for details).
- She must be an excellent example of the breed – in body and temperament.
- She must be more than two years old.

SIRE

Contact the breeder of your bitch for advice on a suitable sire. He or she will know what breeding lines might best suit your bitch. The main concern in all programmes should be temperament and health. Do not use the dog up the road simply because he is convenient – he is unlikely to be of sufficient breeding quality.

The male must be fit, and most importantly, of very good character. If he has been used for stud before, research the character and quality of his offspring before using him. The quality of puppies sired by him previously is a good guide to the quality you can expect in your litter. If your Dobermann is a maiden bitch (virgin), it is advisable to use an experienced stud dog.

It is customary for the bitch to be taken to the stud dog, as the bitch can be aggressive on her own territory and may not accept the dog.

The stud dog must be an excellent specimen of the breed and must also complement your bitch's bloodlines.

SEASON/HEAT

Your bitch, if not spayed, will come into season approximately every six months. The season can be recognised by the swelling of the vulva and the showing of a coloured discharge from the vagina.

The first sight of colour should be noted on your calendar.

Around the tenth day you may want to start pre-mate testing (blood test from your vet) to determine when she should be mated.

THE MATING

It is normal practice for two matings to take place, about 24 hours apart. If possible, before the actual mating, introduce the dog and bitch and allow them to get to know one another. Most males like to court the bitch beforehand. With the initial courting, you can establish if the bitch will need to wear a muzzle, as some can be quite aggressive towards the stud dog.

Talk to your bitch quietly and stroke her gently while the mating takes place. This will give her confidence and help to keep her calm. The dog and the bitch will then 'tie'. This is when the bitch holds the dog, using her internal muscles, and the dog cannot release himself until the bitch relaxes. Some dogs like to turn back-to-back. When the dog ties with the bitch, you should expect a long wait while the sperm from the dog enters into the bitch's uterus. This lasts around 20 to 30 minutes.

Once the mating has been achieved, do not allow your bitch to pass urine for at least two hours, or she may squeeze out some of the precious sperm she has just received.

POST-MATING CARE

Keep your bitch quiet for a few days after the mating and allow her to rest. About four weeks later, your vet may perform an abdominal examination to determine if she is in whelp. Another way of diagnosing pregnancy is by ultrasound scan, which is possible around 30 days after mating.

At this stage, about four weeks into the pregnancy, increase your bitch's food intake. This should be done slowly over a week or so, dividing the meals into two or three throughout the day. The food should be increased by about 25 per cent over the ensuing weeks, and by the end of the pregnancy, she should be having more than double of her usual intake.

Do not stint on feeding her good-quality food; fresh meat and a quality complete biscuit will keep her in good condition. We always give a calcium supplement from about six weeks into the pregnancy along with raspberry-leaf tablets or liquid, as this seems to help the whelping process proceed smoothly. Ask your vet for details.

CHECKLIST

Before the end of pregnancy, ensure you have the following:
• A heat lamp or heat pad.
• Large supply of newspapers.

The brood bitch must be of impeccable temperament.

- Dog-friendly thermometer (substantial, stubby-bulb type).
- Puppy feeding bottle and puppy colostrum or milk.
- Dry towels and kitchen roll.
- Antibacterial and antiviral disinfectant.
- Lubricating gel.
- Weighing scales, note-pad, pen.
- Fleecy veterinary bedding.
- A good supply of washing powder (you'll be surprised how much you will use).
- Have your vet's phone number readily at hand.
- It is courteous to let your vet know in advance when the puppies are due so he can be prepared to attend to your bitch in an emergency.
- Make sure you have booked at least two weeks off work for

after the birth.
- Worming solution/tablets for the puppies and their mother.
- Clean, sharp scissors (to cut the umbilical cord, if necessary).
- Hot-water bottle.

WHELPING BOX

The bitch should be introduced to the whelping box at the beginning of her pregnancy so that she knows it as a safe area for her and her puppies.

The box, made of wood or plastic, should be around 5-6 ft square. The sides should be about 18 inches tall, with a pig-rail running round all of the sides. This rail protects the puppies from being squashed between the box and their mother.

Place newspaper in the whelping box, as it is very absorbent, cheap, and easily disposed of. An overhead heat lamp will be necessary in the early days after the birth to keep the newborn puppies warm. A constant even temperature of around 20 degrees, maintained both day and night, is preferable.

BITCH'S TEMPERATURE

Most pregnancies last 63 days, but some bitches give birth a week early or late. So that you are ready,

start taking your Dobermann's temperature about 10 days before the estimated date of the puppies' arrival. About 24 hours before your Dobermann goes into labour, her temperature will drop by as much as three degrees. A normal temperature for your Dobermann is around 38 to 39 degrees Celsius or 100 to 101 degrees Fahrenheit.

Ask someone to hold your Dobermann steady while you carry out this task.
- Shake the mercury in the thermometer down until it is 36 degrees or lower.
- Place a small amount of lubricating gel on the bulb end of the thermometer.
- Lift the tail and carefully insert the thermometer into the anus (about 2.5cm/1in) and hold it very still.
- Wait around 60 seconds before removing the thermometer and reading it.
- Write down the reading for daily comparison.
- Clean and disinfect after use.
- Never force the thermometer into the rectum.
- If in doubt, do not attempt this procedure.

WHELPING

Towards the end of the pregnancy,

your bitch may be reluctant to eat, and may pass urine (and loose bowel movements) frequently. She may also shiver and shake. The birth is imminent when she starts licking her back end. Straining and pushing will accompany this.

When the puppy is born, allow the bitch to burst the bag that the puppy is encased in. You should only interfere if she is not helping the puppy out. If this is the case, tear the bag away from the pup's mouth, and wipe his nose and mouth to clear away any fluid or mucus, allowing the pup to take its first breath.

If the puppy is not breathing, rub him gently but firmly with a warm, dry towel.

Your bitch will be producing her puppies roughly 30 minutes apart (though it can be up to an hour). Provided she is not distressed and is in no great discomfort, allow her to continue at her own pace. If you are worried at all about your bitch or her puppies, contact your vet for advice.

Make sure you offer your bitch frequent drinks of milk or water with glucose during her labour to keep her hydrated.

Keep a note of the times of the births and whether the placentas came with the puppy. If the placentas are not all accounted for, your vet may need to give her an injection to expel the retained afterbirths to prevent infection and even excessive bleeding.

POST WHELPING

Some Dobermanns take to motherhood very easily but some not so easily. If you are there to give support and a kind word, it helps to build up the bitch's confidence, so consider sleeping near the bitch for the first few days.

In a normal, healthy litter, each new puppy will find his way to the source of milk. This is essential as, for the first few days after the birth, the mother is producing colostrum, which contains the essential protective antibodies necessary to see the puppies through the first few weeks of their lives. So it is vital that every puppy suckles properly and frequently during those first few days.

The area where you house the puppies must be safe and secure (check they cannot get to any electrical cables etc.) Allow a separate area outside the puppy playpen where your bitch can retreat for some well-earned rest.

Good hygiene is of the utmost

importance. Do not allow any strangers or potential new puppy owners to visit the pups without having their shoes and hands sprayed with anti-viral disinfectant.

WEANING

We try to wean our puppies at about three to four weeks of age. The simple rule we follow is to allow as much food as the puppies will clear comfortably, and increase this amount about every three days by about a quarter. Observe the puppies when they are eating as some can be very greedy. If necessary, separate the slower eaters with a dish of their own.

Dobermann puppies are notorious for letting you know when they are ready to take semi-solid or porridge-like food. We have found them on numerous occasions trying to get their teeth into their mother's food, and they show great initiative and determination when doing so.

A contented litter of Dobermann puppies, just four days old.

Long periods of sleep are interspersed with hectic bouts of activity.

A good-quality complete food, fresh meat, and a quality puppy porridge are all essentials for the health and well-being of your new arrivals. Always ensure that there is fresh water available in a shallow non-slip bowl, and that it is replenished on a regular basis.

The puppies should be fed around four or five times a day initially. As they get older, four times a day will be more than sufficient. The number of meals can be gradually decreased as the Dobe puppies grow (see Chapter Two).

POTENTIAL OWNERS

Potential new owners should be invited to visit the litter when it is around five to six weeks of age. It is important always to allow the puppies' mother to see the prospective new owners first, as this will help her to trust them with her pups.

Puppies should not be allowed to go to their new homes until they are at least eight weeks old. You must also ensure that they have been fully weaned from their mother for at least ten days prior to this.

TAILS

In the UK and the US, the Dobermann is a customarily docked breed, and most (but not all) breeders endeavour to have their puppies docked.

Docking is normally performed within the first three days of the birth, by a veterinary surgeon. The tail is usually docked at the first or second vertebrae.

DEWCLAWS

Most breeders have their puppies' dewclaws removed when the tails are docked. This is done by a vet when the puppies are about two days old.

NAILS

Ensure you keep the puppies' nails trimmed every three to four days. Keeping them short will stop them scratching their mother too much, and will help them to get used to being handled later in life.

7 *Health Care*

In many respects, the health of your dog is up to you. If you feed him a well-balanced diet, exercise him regularly, and socialise him well, you will have the makings of a well-conditioned and sociable animal that you can take anywhere.

There is no substitute for knowing your own Dobermann. Over a matter of time, you will get to know his moods, and will know when he is not quite himself. Act on your own instinct. If you have any doubts about your animal's health, do not hesitate to seek a veterinary surgeon's expert advice and help. It is much better to be safe than sorry.

PARASITES

ROUNDWORMS

Regular worming is essential to protect your dog against internal parasites. This will involve the dog being given a liquid or tablet form of treatment available from your vet. There are two types of roundworm that concern us: *Toxocara Canis* and *Toxacaris Leonina*. *Toxocara* is a parasite worm that infects dogs and cats, and can affect humans. Children are most at risk because they often play on ground where dogs have been.

Worms can cause ill health in animals, especially young puppies. Adult dogs do not suffer as badly with the illnesses that worms cause but they contribute more to the spreading of them. Adult roundworms live in the intestine and produce hundreds of eggs feeding off their host. These eggs are passed in your puppy or adult dog's faeces. The eggs are resistant to extreme heat and cold, and can survive up to seven years or more in soil etc.

When you worm your Dobermann, be sure to follow the

directions of the vet and the drug manufacturer. If, after giving the treatment, you feed your Dobermann a small amount of live culture bio-yoghurt (about 100 to 150 mls), mixed with some honey or sugar, you will help prevent any tummy upset that may occur during worming.

Symptoms of roundworm infestation include:

- A dull, harsh coat, thin in appearance and out of condition.
- Pot bellied appearance, or tucked-up abdomen.
- Obvious digestive upset, normally diarrhoea.
- Vomiting and a loss of appetite.
- Listlessness and depression.
- High temperature.
- Convulsions.

Left untreated, your Dobermann can suffer some of these symptoms. The roundworm will migrate from the gut of your animal to the lungs. This can cause lung damage, coughing, and even pneumonia.

TAPEWORMS

Tapeworms have a flat-segmented body and are recognised by single segments or chains (resembling segments of rice) that may be visible in your Dobermann's stool. They can cause weight loss and general debility. Part of the tapeworm lifecycle occurs in the host – the flea – and so treatment against both fleas and tapeworm should be carried out together.

- You should worm your dog regularly - ideally four times a year: autumn, winter, spring and summer.
- Reduce the risk of infection by clearing up after your dog.
- Keep children out of dog runs and where your dog defecates.
- Make sure everyone washes their hands before eating, and don't let children put grass in their mouths.
- Don't share food with your dog (e.g. sweets, biscuits, etc.).
- Use separate dishes for dogs, and wash them up separately.

HEARTWORMS

In some countries, though not in the UK, owners should also treat their dogs for heartworm. Ask your vet for details.

FLEAS

Most dogs have experienced fleas at some time in their lives. Fortunately, Dobermanns do not suffer very often from flea infestation because their short hair and lack of undercoat does not provide the flea with very much protection from the elements.

If you notice your dog scratching, it is possible that he may have picked up an unwanted guest from another animal and may have a reaction to this. Fleas live in the dog's coat and feed on his blood, which may cause the dog to scratch and lick the bitten area, causing intense irritation and eventually leading to sore patches.

Once you have found evidence of fleas, speak to your vet who will prescribe a suitable flea treatment. There are several treatments on the market.

Please remember, if you treat your dog for fleas, you will need to treat the area where he lives – i.e. his bedding, the carpets, and some soft furnishings, couch, chairs, etc. Fleas can also be the carriers of tapeworm eggs, another reason to treat your pet frequently and to be vigilant in their day-to-day care.

MANGE
There are two types of mange, both caused by mites: Sarcoptic and Demodectic.

Sarcoptic mange is highly contagious and spreads easily from dog to dog. It is caused by a microscopic spider-like mite that burrows into the dog's skin. Small, red spots will appear, usually around the neck, ears and on the head. The intense itching causes the dog to scratch the infected area, making those areas become bare, crusty and sore.

A worm-like mite that lives in the hair follicles and the sebaceous glands of the skin causes Demodectic mange. The hair will fall out and puss-filled spots may develop. Demodectic mange is often caught by nursing bitches and can be passed on to her puppies. Your vet can confirm diagnosis by taking skin scrapings from the affected areas and examining them under a microscope. If either of these conditions are diagnosed, your vet will prescribe the appropriate medication.

TICKS
These parasites are picked up when your Dobermann is out exercising, usually in fields or wooded areas, or anywhere near cattle or sheep. The ticks attach themselves firmly to your Dobe's skin and bury their heads underneath. They then feed on his blood, and their bodies become bloated and purplish grey in colour as they gorge themselves.

To remove these parasites without causing further damage to your Dobermann's skin, soak a piece of cotton wool (cotton) in ether, surgical spirit or paraffin, and hold it over the feeding parasite for a few minutes, and the tick will release its hold on the skin. Wipe the puncture area with diluted antiseptic or surgical spirit, and then apply a small amount of antiseptic cream or powder to the affected area.

ACCIDENTS

BURNS
If your Dobermann has been burned by hot or caustic liquid (bleach/acid), wash the affected area immediately with cold water and then apply a greasy ointment such as petroleum jelly. Keep your dog warm to prevent shock, and seek veterinary help at once.

CUTS

Cuts to your dog can be quite common as the smooth coat offers little protection. You can treat any superficial cuts by simple first aid.

Using cotton wool (cotton) soaked in diluted antiseptic solution or warm salt water, wipe and clean the injury carefully. After cleaning, dry the area thoroughly and apply a small amount of antiseptic ointment.

For more serious cuts, cover with a sterile pad or a clean towel, and apply pressure if required to stem the flow of blood, and seek veterinary attention immediately.

HEAT STROKE

This is where your dog's temperature soars to uncontrollable limits, and can lead to collapse, or even seizures. It should be taken very seriously.

Symptoms of heat stroke include the following:
• Heavy panting
• Drowsiness
• Collapse
• Frothing at the mouth
• Distress.

In such instances, you should carry out the following:

- Remove the dog to a cool, shaded area and the nearest water supply.
- Clear any froth from around the dog's mouth.
- Dowse the whole dog in cold water.
- Seek veterinary help immediately.

Never leave dogs in cars – whatever the weather. Many dogs have died of heat stroke in cars, even when it has been cloudy or overcast, and even if the owner has left a window open for them.

POISONING

If you suspect your dog has eaten a poisonous substance, do not waste any time wondering what it could be, seek veterinary assistance straightaway. If the poison is on

your dog's coat and is clearly visible, wash it off immediately to prevent your dog from licking at it and thereby ingesting it. Take a small amount of the substance in a container to the vet's, as he may need to identify it in order to decide on a course of action.

Signs of poisoning include:
- Acute vomiting
- Collapse or even unconsciousness
- Muscle twitching
- Convulsions
- General weakness
- Bleeding from the back passage, mouth or gums.

COMMON AILMENTS

BLOAT (GASTRIC TORSION)
Gastric torsion mainly occurs in deep-chested dogs, such as Greyhounds, Great Danes, Mastiffs and Dobermanns, etc. The cause of this distressing condition is many faceted. The main symptoms are the blowing up of the stomach, with associated vomiting of frothy, slimy mucus.

The dog can be very distressed and cry with pain. This is because the stomach and/or the spleen can twist, causing the stomach to be unable to empty its contents into the small bowel. Fermentation can

result and the build-up of the gases can blow the stomach out, making it turn round on itself, sometimes taking the spleen with it. This is a veterinary emergency and needs to be treated immediately.

Some suggestions to try to avoid this condition are as follows:
- Do not exercise your dog after feeding him; give him a few hours to digest some of his food.
- Try not to let him bolt his food down in one; feed him twice a day if possible, ensuring the food is soaked.
- Watch how much water he drinks, as too much can also cause bloating.

CARDIOMYOPATHY
Cardiomyopathy is known as the silent killer in Dobermanns. It affects the heart muscle of adult Dobes. There are two main types of heart abnormality: disturbances in the heart rhythm (arrhythmias), and weakening of the heart muscle itself.

Dogs that suffer from this disease can present with various symptoms and signs, but all have cardiac arrhythmias in common, a very irregular heart beat.

Some subtle changes in your

dog may be noticeable: intolerance of strenuous activity, lethargy, weight loss and intermittent coughing. However, to all intents and purposes, the dog may look healthy enough, and then suddenly collapse and die in front of you. This can happen during exercise, at rest, or even during sleep, but most frequently while running or walking.

If caught early enough, this disease can be treated to make the animal more comfortable, but unfortunately cannot be cured.

The exact cause of Cardiomyopathy is unknown, but there are ongoing surveys in the UK which have suggested that there is a genetic origin.

EYE PROBLEMS

Some Dobermanns have rather deep-set eyes and loose eyelids. This can sometimes be a problem as it is easier for a foreign body to

get trapped between the eyelids and cause infection. Any mucus that accumulates within the corner of the eye will need removing, as this could cause infection.

Many Dobermanns will develop cataracts in their later years. Cataracts are seen as opaque areas on the lens, which can diminish a dog's vision, but it is not necessary to treat them.

During the last decade, it has been reported that there is an eye condition known as PHPV – Persistent Hyperplastic Vitreous.

The clinical symptoms of this disease can only be detected by the use of a slit-lamp bio-microscope. Through it, you can see small fibrovascular pigment dots on the back of the lens. These dots do not interfere with the vision of the dog, nor do they cause problems in later years.

Dutch vet Dr Stades researched the disease and developed a grading system (ask your vet or breed club for details), advising that dogs with a grade II result or higher should not be bred from.

HIP DYSPLASIA

Hip dysplasia is a condition of the hip joints. Malformation or displacement of the hip joint can mean that the ball and socket connection fits badly. Ultimately, this can cause the head of the femur (the ball) to rub on the edge of the joint (the socket), which inevitably causes arthritis in the hip joint.

The major sign of a limb disorder is a recurring limp that may be intermittent in its presence, or it may become more severe after exercise. If you are at all concerned about your Dobermann, consult your vet, who can confirm diagnosis by X-raying the hips.

Even though there have been numerous surveys into hip dysplasia, there is no real evidence as to why this disease occurs. Many people think it may be multifactorial in its causes. Nutrition, genetic causes, over exercise of young stock, or even over supplementation of calcium etc., have been cited as having some influence in this condition.

The degree of displacement can be measured and given a score. Ask your vet for details of your country's testing scheme.

KENNEL COUGH

This infection is most prevalent during the summer. It is highly contagious to other dogs, and can be passed on at shows, in kennels,

or even at your veterinary surgery where another infected dog has been. Prevention can take the form of vaccination.

The virus is airborne in droplet form either from an infected animal's breath or from sputum (via coughing). Young puppies and older dogs are most at risk.

Symptoms include a continual harsh, dry or mucus cough, lack of appetite, nasal or eye discharge, lethargy (general lack of interest, lying around). A whooping-cough type of sound can identify kennel cough.

If your dog shows these signs, the illness will be severe and you should consult your veterinary surgeon as soon as possible. If left untreated it could cause damage to the respiratory system, which may eventually be fatal. Cough mixture, along with antibiotics, may be needed to treat this disease, as prescribed by your vet.